Alexander, the Great

Sumitha Menon

Alexander, the Great
© *New Horizon Media*

First Edition: April 2009
80 Pages
Printed in India.

ISBN 978–81–8493–136–5
Pro–ya–en–37

Prodigy Books
177/103, First Floor,
Ambal's Building, Lloyds Road,
Royapettah, Chennai 600 014.
Ph: +91-44-4200-9603

Email : support@nhm.in
Website : www.nhm.in

Prodigy Books is an imprint of New Horizon Media Private Limited

CONTENTS

Birth of a Warrior

All of you would have heard of Alexander the Great. But how much do you really know about him? Do you think he deserves the title that follows his name? Let us explore through these pages the adventurous journey of this young, legendary king.

Alexander's claims to fame are his military achievements. He is considered by far as the greatest military genius of all time. His life is an amazing tale of honour, power, scandal and bravery.

In 356 B.C., baby Alexander was born in Pella, the capital of Macedon, which was a kingdom of ancient Greece where his father Philip was the king. His mother

Olympias was a beautiful princess from a country called Epirus, just outside Macedonia. His father, King Philip II had married several times (which was allowed in those days). He had other children but Alexander was special. His brilliant military conquests earned him a place in history.

At the time of Alexander's birth, his father was on a victorious military campaign, capturing an important town. According to the Greek historian Plutarch, three messages reached King Phillip at the same time. The first one was that Parmenion, one of his generals, had defeated Macedon's historic enemies, the Illyrians. The second informed that one of his racehorses had won at the Olympic Games. The third message was that a son was born to him. Thus Alexander was born into a state that was already in the midst of great change.

The name Alexander was common in the Macedonian royal house. Both Alexander's parents were said to have descended from great mythical heroes of ancient Greece—Philip from Heracles (Hercules), son of the god Zeus, and Olympias from Achilles, one of the heroes of the Trojan War. So the ancient Greeks believed that Alexander, being the son of the descendents of gods and heroes, was sure to achieve greatness.

Alexander's mother, Olympias, was an ambitious, determined lady and short-tempered too. In the eyes of the Macedonians, she was a strange, exotic woman. She was a glamorous queen, but had a cruel streak in her character. Quarrelsome and bad-tempered, she demanded respect. She was a follower of mystic cults of the gods Orpheus and Dionysus. She used to have snakes as pets and engaged in mystical ceremonies, involving frenzied dancing with her pet snakes. Her weird hobbies did not appeal to Philip and put a strain on their marriage.

But both Philip and Olympias loved Alexander very much and wanted to see him grow up fit to be a king. One of Philip's other wives had given him a son called Arrhidaeus, but he had a mental disability. This made Alexander the favourite to succeed Philip. Also, Olympias with her forceful personality was determined that it would be so. The disagreements in the family atmosphere definitely would have had an impact on Alexander's development. Under Philip, Macedonia grew and flourished and with Philip away on campaigns most of the time, the mutual dislike between his parents deepened further.

So Alexander's mother was the guiding force during his formative years. She instilled in him the idea that he was destined to ascend to great heights. She also may have tried to distance and turn him against his strict father, specially pointing out his moral shortcomings. Hence it was no wonder that while Alexander had great regard for his mother, in spite of her unprincipled actions, the father and son disliked each other. Yet Alexander genuinely admired his father for his military exploits and in many ways followed his footsteps as a military leader and king.

Unfortunately, there is not much written about Alexander's early years. He might have spent a lot of time playing in the corridors and gardens of the palace at Pella. Most accounts paint him as an extremely intelligent boy, adept at wrestling and fighting, archery and javelin. He had a particular aptitude for horsemanship. Swimming was one sport that eluded him. Even at a very young age, he would be seen in the company of great politicians, artists and generals; he learned a lot from them. Once during his father's absence, he entertained the ambassadors from the king of Persia and impressed them with his gracious and friendly manner. He amicably entered into a conversation with them and asked them questions which were far from childish or trifling. His questions included the nature of the road into inner Asia, the character of their king, how he dealt with the enemies and what forces he brought to the field and so on. The guests were full of admiration for the young boy and surmised that his forwardness and high purpose put him a step above his father Philip.

Whenever Alexander heard that his father had won an important victory, instead of rejoicing at it wholly, he would tell his friends that his father with his conquests would leave him and them no opportunities for performing illustrious actions. He was more inclined for action and glory rather than pleasure or riches and looked upon his father's achievements as an obstacle for his own future achievements. He would have preferred to succeed to a kingdom involved in troubles and wars, which would give him ample opportunity to exercise his courage and enhance his honour. He believed that an already settled and vast inheritance would only lead to an inactive life and mere enjoyment of wealth and luxury.

A Princely Life

In 344 B.C., when he was 12 years old, an incident happened that won Alexander a lot of respect. The grassy plains of Thessaly, south of Macedon, are famous for wild horses. A horse-dealer brought Bucephalus, a magnificent black stallion to Philip, offering to sell him for the great sum of 13 silver talents. In Alexander's time, a skilled labourer made only about 2 to 3 drachmas a day and 6,000 drachmas were required to make 1 talent. That worker would have to slog for 100 years before he could think of buying this horse. However they went into the field to try him out, but they found him very ferocious and unmanageable. He reared up whenever someone tried to mount him and could not bear to hear the voice of any of Philip's attendants. Every one dismissed him as a useless and disobedient creature and Philip refused to buy him. Alexander who stood nearby said, 'What an excellent horse do they lose for want of address and boldness to manage him!' Philip first ignored what he had said. But when he repeated it several times, he scolded him for criticizing the decision of the older people.

'I could manage this horse,' replied Alexander, 'better than others do.'

'And if you do not,' said Philip, 'what will you forfeit for your rashness?'

'I will pay,' answered Alexander, 'the whole price of the horse.' At this the whole group started laughing. Finally every one agreed to the wager.

Alexander immediately ran to the horse. He had noticed that the horse was scared by the sight of his own shadow. He took hold of the bridle and turned him directly towards the sun, thus turning the horse's head away from its shadow. He stood near the horse, stroking him gently and gradually calmed him down. When he found the horse slowly becoming eager and fiery, he mounted him. When comfortably seated, he slowly and tenderly controlled him without striking or spurring him. Soon he found all the rebelliousness displayed by the horse had vanished and was replaced by an impatient longing to let go. Alexander let him gallop at full speed, rousing him with a commanding voice. Philip and his friends first looked on anxiously, worried about the outcome. But when they saw him return, triumphant and overjoyed, they burst out cheering and applauding. His father, shedding tears of joy, kissed him and said, 'O my son, look thee out a kingdom equal to and worthy of thyself, for Macedonia is too little for thee.' ('My son, ask yourself another kingdom, for that which I leave you is too small for you.')

The horse was with him for almost twenty years, serving him as a war horse and hunter. In 326 B.C., during the battle of the River Hydaspes in the Punjab in modern Pakistan, Bucephalus was injured and died. Alexander personally led the funeral procession and buried him with full honours. He built a city named Bucephala after his friend, but no trace of the city has been found. Throughout history, Alexander was the only king to name a city after a horse.

King Philip was often away from Pella either on diplomatic missions or was busy conquering neighbouring states; so young Alex was more in the company of his mother. Olympias used every opportunity to fuss over her son. But she also employed home tutors to help him with his education. His first tutor was Leonidas—a tough, little man and a stickler for rules. He acted like a foster-father to Alexander. Leonidas took upon himself to toughen Alex up and enforced brisk early-morning runs and a strict diet. Leonidas would hunt through Alex's belongings in case his mother had given him any forbidden treats.

One story goes that once, in offering a sacrifice, Alexander burnt two whole handfuls of incense in the altar-fire. Leonidas ticked him off saying, 'When you've conquered the spice-bearing regions, you can throw away all the incense you like. Till then, don't waste it.' Years later, Alexander conquered Asia—the region where incense and other exotic spices came from. Along with the usual gifts for his mother and sister, he sent Leonidas a consignment of 18 tons of precious frankincense and myrrh—the resale of which would make him enormously rich. He told him that there was no longer any need to be stingy to the gods. His action, on the one hand demonstrates his generous nature, though in a mocking manner. It also reveals Alexander's capacity for holding grudges. He was never one to forget an insult or injury. He waited patiently to carry out his vengeance.

In spite of Leonidas's strictness, Alex found time for his hobbies, including hunting and music-making. Like his hero Hercules, Alex too was a keen hunter. He was fond of stick-fighting and was a fast runner. He enjoyed drama and poetry. He liked to play the lyre (an instrument a bit like a small harp). But like swimming, music was not his forte. He had a tutor for lyre lessons, but there was no improvement. A story goes that Alex once asked his music tutor whether it really mattered whether he played one particular note than the other. The teacher told him that for future kings it did not matter, but for musicians it did matter—a polite and careful hint that music was not for him.

When Alexander was 13, Philip decided to send him away to school in the countryside, along with some other children from the Macedonian families. Philip not only wanted to give his son the best education that money could buy, but also wanted his son to be away from his mother who was bent on spoiling him.

Under Aristotle's Tutelage

As Alexander's tutor, Philip appointed Aristotle (from Athens)—who was one of the foremost Greek philosophers of his day. The result was the birth of one of the most famous mentor-student relationships in history. Apart from being a great teacher, Aristotle's family connection was also taken into account. His father had served as court physician to an earlier Macedonian king. Also Aristotle had previously served in the court of Hermeias in Atarneus and an alliance there would be useful for Philip's plans to invade Persia.

For Aristotle, it was a great honour and also a chance to pursue his research under the most powerful of the Greek states.

Philip exhorted his son to work hard and to learn to avoid making the mistakes that he himself had made. Alexander was more concerned about the future conflicts over succession to his father's throne because of the number of step-brothers he had. Alexander's ambition was evident even at this age.

Among the lessons Aristotle taught were the following: Medicine, Natural History (Biology), Geography, Politics, Greek Literature, Physics, Astronomy, Philosophy and Rhetoric (how to make fantastic speeches and win arguments by using words cleverly). Aristotle was very interested in science, especially Botany and Zoology and passed on his enthusiasm to his young pupil. It accounts for Alexander's fascination for the exotic plants and animals that he saw in Asia in his later life. When Alexander set off on his invasion of Asia, he took along with him a large group of zoologists and botanists who collected materials and information for scientific research. He also owed to Aristotle his inclination to practise the art of medicine. When any of his friends were sick, he would always prescribe their course of diet and the right medicines for their disease. Alexander learnt a lot from Aristotle and his influence on Alexander's life and growth was enormous.

Aristotle gave Alexander a copy of the epic *Iliad*, written on a papyrus scroll. The *Iliad* was written by the Greek poet Homer, and it narrated the story of the Trojan wars between Greece and the city of Troy. The wars had begun with the abduction of the Greek Queen Helen by Paris, the Trojan prince. Alexander was so fascinated by the description of the battle-scenes and the gallant heroes that he preserved the scroll all his life. In fact, Alexander began to model himself on some of the Greek heroes, seeing himself as a second Achilles. He might have been encouraged in this by another of his tutors Lysimachus whom Alexander was very fond of. This teacher called him Achilles instead of Alexander, implying that through his mother he was related to the super-hero.

As Alexander grew up, he had to take two challenging tests to prove himself a worthy successor to his father. The first one was to kill a wild boar and the second was to kill a man in battle. Once victorious in these tasks, he would be considered a man and could wear a special belt to show this. He would be allowed to lie back rather than sit upright at the symposia[1]—the all-male parties that were common at the Macedonian court.

Killing a wild boar was easy for Alexander. After that he became a keen hunter, fighting lions, bears and other wild animals. It was only when he was about 14 years old, that he had the chance to kill a man in battle. Though only in his teens Alexander, having passed the tests of manhood, was considered to be a man.

Sculptures of Alexander show that, though not very tall, he was a handsome young man—very strong and fit. Alexander was a fast runner and once was asked whether he would run a race in the Olympic Games. He said he would, if he would have kings to race with him. He seems to have looked with indifference upon the professional athletes. Alexander inherited his passion and strong will from his mother, while from his father he imbibed a hard-headed, realistic approach to life and courage and ability to make quick decisions. This mix of skills made Alexander an extraordinary man. Like most powerful people in Greece, Alexander visited Delphi to consult the priestess of the oracle. It was believed that she could predict the future. The priestess is said to have told him, 'Young man, you are invincible.'

To the Greeks, all non-Greeks were known as 'barbarians.' Aristotle asserted his influence to instil this idea into Alexander. Persian civilization was in fact as old as and as interesting and impressive as that of the Greeks. However, Aristotle drilled into Alexander that the Persians were barbarians who deserved to be conquered and made slaves by the Greeks. He therefore encouraged Alexander to be a leader of the Greeks, but a despot to the barbarians. Aristotle saw barbarians as pleasure-seekers, weak-willed and soft. Persians, according to him, got carried away and did things to excess, while the Greeks did everything in moderation. Alexander, in order to be a great hero, naturally placed great value on honour, with its virtues of self-control and self-denial. So in his own life, he did not eat or drink too much, gave generously, keeping little for himself. Alexander spent three years studying with the great philosopher.

[1] *The details of the symposium make interesting reading. It took place after the evening meal had ended. About 30 men attended (no women were allowed), each wearing a garland and lying on a couch on his left elbow. Discussion ranged from politics to love, and wine was served. Prayers brought events to a close. The men then paraded drunkenly through the streets before going to bed.*

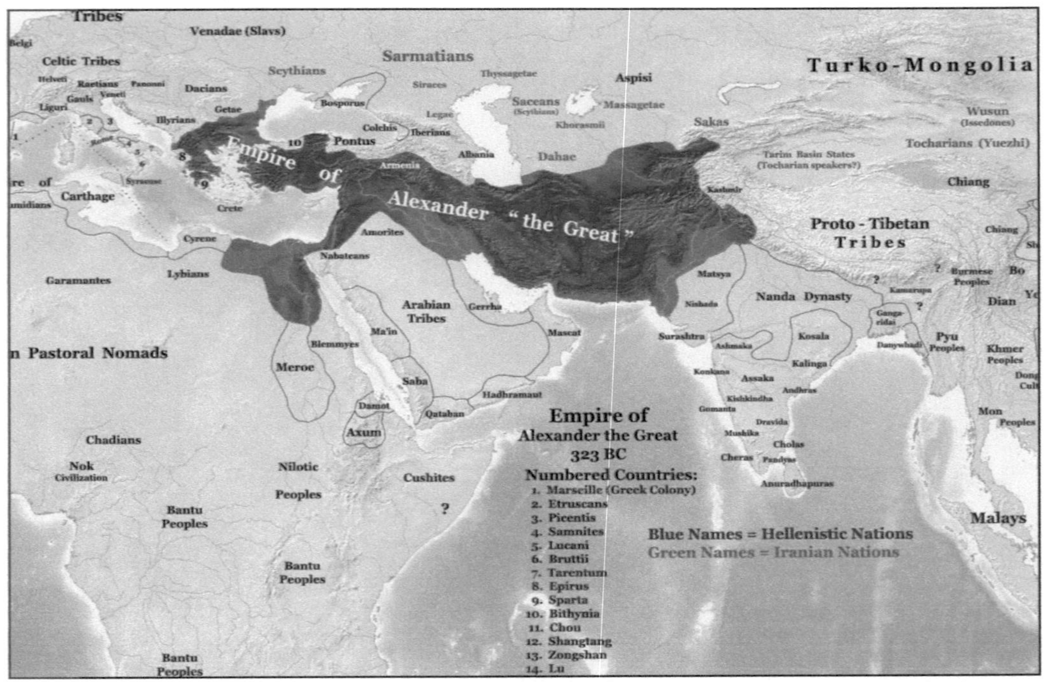

Alexander's Empire

The Road to Kingship

In 340 B.C. when Alexander was 16, he had finished school. His father thought that Alex was ready for more responsibility. So Philip summoned him to return and serve as Regent of Macedonia and Master of the Royal Seal, when he went away on military campaign against two eastern Greek cities—Byzantium and Perinthus.

Antipater, an old family friend was appointed to advise him, but Alexander, happy to be in charge, loved every minute of it. Immediately after Philip's departure, a rebellion broke out among the Maedi, the fierce and powerful tribe that lived in Thrace. Eager for action, Alexander himself went to suppress the rebels and turned the city into a military outpost for Macedonia, which he renamed as Alexandropolis. In 339 B.C., war broke out between Macedon and the powerful city-state of Athens. Almost a year later, Philip defeated the Greek forces led by Athens and Thebes at the battle of Chaeronea.

Alexander was in command of the army that faced the Thebans. His responsibility was great, because the Thebans were better trained. He proved his bravery in the battlefield. This early bravery made Philip so fond of him that it pleased him to hear his people call him their general while Alexander was referred to as king.

Philip, in a grand gesture of magnanimity, released 2,000 Athenian prisoners and announced that he would send the ashes of the 1,000 Athenian soldiers to their home city of Athens. Moreover, Alexander was given the job of carrying out this important mission. It meant that Philip himself was indirectly proclaiming to the Greeks that Alexander was their future king.

After this great victory, Philip became the undisputed leader of all Greece. He began to organize the league of Corinth to unite the many Greek states under his leadership to maintain peace. He also planned a major expedition against the Persian Empire. Persia had invaded Greece in 480–79 B.C. The humiliating Persian invasion was a sore point with many Greeks. Also, the king of Persia had fabulous wealth and the thought of getting a share of it was indeed an attractive prospect.

Unfortunately, while Philip was engaged in making peace with the Greek states, his own family was in the midst of a dreadful row. Philip had fallen out with Olympias and proclaimed his marriage to Euridice, a young Macedonian girl and the niece of one of his generals. At the marriage, Eurydice's uncle proposed a toast to the new couple, hoping that she would give the kingdom a lawful successor. This irritated Alexander so much that he left the party in anger. He along with his mother left the country. Leaving his mother with relatives in Epirus, Alexander went into hiding in Illyria.

Demaratus, an old friend of the family, reproached Philip for creating so many dissensions and calamities in the house. Philip sent for his son and, by Demaratus's mediation, Alexander came home.

Olympias continued to be in exile. Philip worried that Olympias would persuade her brother, the king of Epirus, to make trouble against him. To seal the friendship, Philip offered his own daughter, Cleopatra (one of Alex's sisters), in marriage to King Epirus.

Olympias came for the wedding. There was a grand banquet, with a lot of feasting and drinking. Everyone seemed to be having a good time. On the second day of the celebrations, Philip was walking in a ceremonial procession, when he was stabbed by a member of his own body guards. The assassin was caught and killed on the spot. His name was Pausanias. It was said that he had a row with Philip and had taken revenge. Fingers were pointed at Olympias who might have instigated Pausanias to commit the crime. Some others put the blame on Alexander also since he stood to benefit the most by his father's death, as Philip had chosen him to be his successor.

The end result was that at the age of 20, Alexander became King Alexander of Macedon and ruler of all Greece.

At the Helm

Alexander succeeded to a kingdom beset on all sides with dangers and enemies. Though Philip had conquered many states, he had no time to fully conquer all of them and get them accustomed to his ways. So there was general disorder and confusion. Alexander had the help of two important people—his trusted adviser Antipater and his top general Parmenio. With their support, he acted hastily to make sure that the throne was his. The Macedonian army also pledged support to him. He killed all his political opponents and possible rivals to the throne. He, however, spared the life of his half-brother, Philip Arrhidaeus, who was mentally ill. He went south to take over the League of Corinth, as his father's successor. Though Alexander was brave and had brilliant tactics, his ruthlessness was another reason for his success. He was going to be king and he was not going to let anyone stand in his way.

To win the support of the Macedonian people and to maintain his hold over the foreign states, he publicly announced assuring the people that he would rule the states on the same principles that his father had followed. As a liberal measure, he removed direct taxation on the Macedonian citizens.

Another method he adopted to gain land was to marry and make allies. Alexander married three times. He first married Roxanne, the beautiful daughter of the chieftain Oxyartes. His lands lay on the route from Persia to India. The marriage took place in 327 B.C., when Alexander was 29. Roxanne gave birth to a son, who later came to be known as Alexander IV. Like his marriage to Roxanne, his other two marriages also improved diplomatic ties. One marriage was to Stateira, one of the daughters of the defeated and assassinated Darius III of Persia. The other marriage was to Parysatis, a daughter of Artaxerxes III, one of Darius's predecessors.

Alexander had great regard for his two friends. His closest and most trusted friend was Hephaestion, whom he had met while studying under Aristotle. Hephaestion was his body guard, adviser and the grand vizier of his empire. He died in 324 B.C. in Ecbatana (in modern-day Iran). Alexander gave him a ceremonious burial.

His other close friend was Bagoas, a young Persian boy, whom Alexander met in 330 B.C. Bagoas remained with him throughout his life. But for these two friendships, Alexander was a loner whose passion was adventure and conquest and not love.

After Philip's death, there followed a wave of rebellions against Macedonia in Greece and among her northern neighbours. No one had suspected that Alexander was going to be even tougher than his father. They had considered it an opportunity to gain back their freedom from the Macedonian rule. Alexander acted with speed, leading his army up and down Greece, crushing rebellions left, right and centre. His brilliance and the clever tactics he used to get out of difficult situations astonished many. Thessaly, Thrace, Triballia and the Paeonians across the River Danube—all were soon part of Macedonia. He next turned to the west to defeat the Illyrians. Macedon was now secure.

However, the Greek partners in the League of Corinth were not to be trusted. A false rumour that Alexander had died on military campaign had been spread and a number of states, led by Thebes, rose in revolt. Immediately, Alexander led his army to Thebes, covering 300 miles in 12 days and the Macedonian army soon captured Thebes. Alexander was often merciless towards his enemies. His army rampaged through the streets, looting, plundering and causing blood-shed. Thebes was one of the most historic cities in Greece, but Alexander saw to it that every building was wiped out. To teach a cruel lesson to the Thebans, he killed 6,000 Thebans and sold 30,000 as slaves. Thebes totally disappeared from the map and Greece was firmly under his control.

He forced the Greek states to do three things:

1. Renew the League set up by his father.

2. Pledge their loyalty to him.

3. Agree to press on with Philip's plans for an attack on the Persian Empire.

Meanwhile his mother Olympias was taking care of the affairs at Pella when Alexander was away. She showed her vengeful side by killing Caranus, the son of Philip and Euridice. She killed his sister and mother too. The cruelty of the murders shocked most people, including Alexander himself.

Any way, it was with relief that Alexander returned to Pella. He had terrified the Greek city-states into obedience to him at last. He was now ready to embark on the greatest adventure of his life. It was time for him to take up where his father had left off.

Early Conquests

Alexander immediately began his plans for the invasion. Alexander had practical reasons also for hurrying up with the mission. Philip had left him in immense debt. His army was expensive to maintain. He did manage to tide over the difficulties with more loans and gifts, but the wealth of the Persian Empire was the best proposition to his financial problems.

Like his father, Alexander used to say that he was going on the Asian war expedition with a vast 'Greek' army, but actually it was 90 per cent Macedonian. Though most of the Greeks apparently offered support to Alexander, many states were planning to stir up trouble in his absence. To try preventing this, he appointed his trusted adviser Antipater to be in charge of Macedonia while he was away. He left part of the Macedonian army to suppress any rebellion.

The army that Alexander had under him was itself a marvellous achievement, technically and theoretically near-perfect. The land forces of nearly 50,000 were divided into 43,000 of infantry and 6,000 of cavalry. Although it was said to be a Greek war against the Persian Empire, quite a few Greeks had actually joined the Persian army to fight as mercenaries. Mercenaries are soldiers who fight only for money. They are willing to fight for another country (even on the enemy's side) provided they are paid for it. The Persian king's fabulous wealth attracted many Greek soldiers to join his army. The result was that non-Macedonian Greeks were more in the Persian army than in the Greek army.

In the spring of the year 334 B.C. Alexander set off to Thrace and sailed across the narrow Hellespont waterway that separated Greece from Persian-controlled Asia. Alexander had packed everything into about 100 huge ships and made sacrifices to the gods for a safe journey before sailing. He steered the ship himself. When he was half-way across he sacrificed a bull to Poseidon, god of the sea. As he approached the land, he threw his spear hard into the sand and jumped onto the shore fully armoured. He set up altars on the shore for his heroes Heracles and to the gods Athena and Zeus.

His next journey was to the ancient city of Troy, which was in ruins. There he and his friend Hephaistion offered more sacrifices at the tombs of Achilles and his loyal friend Patroclus. Once his duties were over, he began his march east towards the enemy.

Alexander was just 21, when he landed in Asia. He had been king of Macedon for less than two years. His dream conquest lay in front of him with many battles and victories. His landing in Asia also marked another turning point in his life—he was never to see his native land again.

Meanwhile in Babylon, Persian King Darius III and his officers were planning their move. Among his senior officers was Memnon of Rhodes, a brilliant Greek general who had fallen out with King Philip some years before and joined the Persian side as a mercenary. The Persian Empire stretched from the Mediterranean Sea in the east to modern-day Pakistan and from the Aral Sea in the north to Egypt in the south. The Persians decided to confront Alexander before he moved further away from the coast.

Alexander, the Great

In May finally the two sides met across the River Granicus, just east of Troy. Alexander's experienced officers such as Parmenio knew that they were at a disadvantage. The Persians had the advantage of higher ground and would wait for Alexander to make the first move. It would be difficult to cross the fast-flowing river and climb her muddy banks. The Macedonian army would soon be defeated. They persuaded Alexander to wait until nightfall. They left their campfires burning to fool the Persians and moved to a better crossing-point, in the darkness of the night, further downstream.

In the morning Alexander rode Bucephalus, leading the charge across the river. The Macedonian army outnumbered the Persian army of 16,000 infantry and 15,000 cavalry. Persians were no match for the Macedonians in open battle and Alexander easily had his first victory in Asia. However, he was nearly killed by Spithridates, satrap of Ionia. Spithridates was about to strike the final blow with his axe, when Cleitus, brother of Alexander's childhood nurse, saved him by cutting off the Persian's arm.

Alexander moved his men further east, down the Aegean coast of Asia Minor. Most Greek cities, happy to be liberated from Persian rule, welcomed him. And as his army passed through each important state, he left a troop of his soldiers behind to show who the boss was. Macedonian officers replaced the local Persian rulers (deputies of the Great King known as satraps). Many coastal cities gave in without a fight but a few resisted. One was Miletus and the other was Halicarnassus, whose defence was led by Memnon of Rhodes who arrived by sea along with the Persian fleet. The Persians had some early victories. They fought valiantly and almost overpowered the Macedonians but eventually Alexander captured the city with the help of a local Queen Ada, who was living in exile. She adopted him as her son and joined her faction with Alexander. Together they forced Memnon to withdraw from the city by sea. Most of the city was burnt down. Alexander made Ada the queen to rule the state on his behalf and she was indeed grateful to him.

Macedonians lost many of their men in the above battle. The only satisfaction was that they had secured another naval base.

Vanquishing King Darius

Memnon was soon preparing for a revenge attack on Greece itself. It would have caused a lot of problems to Alexander, but as luck would have it Memnon fell ill and died suddenly of fever. As a result, the Persians dropped their plans to attack Greece. This stroke of luck convinced Alexander that he was Fortune's favourite.

Alexander marched his troops towards east. At a place called Gordium he met up with the first batch of troops, sent from home for reinforcement. Here, there was an antique wagon, said to have belonged to the legendary King Midas (the greedy king of Greek Mythology who was granted his wish that everything he touches be turned to gold). The yoke of the wagon was tied to a tall pole, with a huge and complicated knot. The ends of the knots were tucked away, making it impossible to untie it. According to ancient legends, it was prophesied by a local oracle that whoever managed to untie the knot would become the master of Asia.

Alexander rose to the challenge. He never wasted an opportunity to prove himself in any competition. He was determined to show every one that he was the one destined to rule over Asia.

The knot in the thick rope was not an easy one. It was extremely complicated and many had failed in their attempts. It needed a lot of patience and skill. However, Alexander had his own way of solving the problem. He simply drew the sword and cut open the knot with a single stroke. It might not have been what the oracle had in mind. But it showed that the conqueror of Asia had arrived.

Alexander again began his march eastwards to meet Darius and the Persians. But the Great King Darius himself was charging west. So the two armies missed each other. Darius stumbled upon a few Macedonians who were sick and wounded—left behind in a makeshift camp. He treated them horribly. First he cut off their hands so that they could never fight again. Then he sent them on a tour of his fierce Iranian cavalry, waiting to charge in the coming battle. Darius then sent them to Alexander so that they may report to him what they had seen.

The Macedonian prisoners finally found their own army, but their condition was sad and pathetic. The army had been marching for two days, covering 70 miles, only to find that Darius and his men had overtaken them and were already occupying a strategic position. The Persians had cut Alexander's supply lines. There was heavy downpour and the Macedonian army was caught in it. They were fully drenched and exhausted. Furthermore, they saw what Darius had done to their comrades and heard their vivid account of the vastness of the Persian forces. It was enough to demoralize most of them. Alexander somehow managed to boost their morale and got his soldiers ready for another combat.

The Persian army, commanded by Darius himself, was larger than Alexander's army. Though less in numbers, Alexander knew how to use even a weak situation to his advantage. He stretched his right wing much further out than the left wing of his enemies. He led from the front and fought the barbarians. Alexander's well-trained army was superior and forced the barbarians to flee. Alexander was wounded in the thigh during the battle against Darius with whom he fought face-to-face. However, this big battle against the Persians at Issus was a great victory for Alexander. He had overthrown above hundred thousand of his enemies, except for Darius who escaped narrowly by fleeing from the scene. Alexander however took his chariot and his bow and returned from pursuing him.

It might look a little strange that a great king such as Darius should run away, but he knew that the important thing was to stay alive. He could still reorganize his army and fight Alexander another day. And as long as he was alive, Alexander could not claim to be the master of Asia.

The flight of Darius, however, gave Alexander a taste of the high life of the king. His men, plundering through the barbarians' camp, found them exceedingly rich. They were full of gold, silver, weapons and grand oriental tapestries. They reserved Darius's tent for Alexander, which was full of splendid furniture and large quantities of gold and silver. When Alexander arrived he decided to cleanse himself of the toils of the war in the Great King's own bathtub. Here he saw the bathing vessels, the water-pots, the pans, and the ointment boxes, all made of gold and the whole place was exquisitely perfumed. Then he changed into the splendid bath robes of Darius and walked into a pavilion of great size and height. The couches and tables there were perfectly magnificent. Preparations for an entertainment were grandly done. Alexander had all the captured royal gold spread out before him and then he stretched out on the royal couch for a sumptuous feast. Turning to his dining companions, he said, 'This, it seems, is royalty.'

While Alexander was having dinner after the battle of Issus, he came to know that Darius's mother and wife and two unmarried daughters were among the rest of the prisoners. They were wailing, because they had seen Darius's empty chariot and thought he was dead. Alexander informed them that Darius was alive and that they need not fear any harm from Alexander himself. He made it clear to them that his desire was to dominate over the land. He ordered his men to provide Darius's family with everything they had been used to. He also allowed them to bury the Persians and to take for themselves whatever garments or furniture from the booty he had collected. He instructed that they be given proper attention and respect. He allowed larger pension for their maintenance than before. His humane and generous attitude impressed the women.

After the battle of Issus, the Macedonian army received considerable part of the booty that made them all sufficiently rich. This gave the Macedonians a taste of the Persian wealth and their extravagant grandeur of living and soon they were only too eager to go further. However, Alexander, before he proceeded any further, had plenty to do. He had to capture several ports that offered shelter and supplies for the Persian fleet, before he had complete control of the coastal area known as Phoenicia (modern Israel). The city of Tyre, however, refused to surrender.

The main part of Tyre (known as New Town) was built behind massive walls on a small island, half a mile off the coast where the Old town stood. Alexander had no navy, capable of doing any damage at that range. However, he came up with another plan. He built a causeway (platform) to the island to attack it. When this was destroyed, he built another. Again luck favoured Alexander. A number of nearby towns and cities surrendered to the Macedonian army and gave Alexander the use of their ships. Finally he managed to attack the island from the seaward side. After a siege that had lasted for seven months, Alexander took possession of the city in 332 B.C.

The capture of Tyre was a great achievement. The platform that Alexander's men built across the sea has not been destroyed. The modern city of Tyre now stands on its foundations. To warn others who resisted, he executed about 2,000 Tyrian soldiers and more than thousands of civilians were either killed or sold into slavery.

Invasion of Egypt

Alexander continued his journey south and after a long siege captured Gaza. To teach a lesson to others, he ordered the imprisoned Arab governor to be tied to a chariot and dragged around the city walls until he died.

For his next target, which was Egypt, Alexander headed towards the west. The ancient land of pyramids and pharaohs had fascinated Alexander ever since he had read about it as a boy. Egypt was also valued for its important location and for its vast wealth of gold, grain and other goods. The land also posed a challenge, as it was surrounded by deserts on three sides. Luckily Alexander did not have to do any fighting there, because the Egyptians welcomed him as their liberator from Persian rule.

Egypt was well known for its ancient civilization, one that the Egyptians were really proud of. For the past 200 years, however, it had been ruled by Persians, who followed a different religion. Alexander had now freed them from the oppressive rule of the Persians and he was no less than a hero to them.

Alexander respected the Egyptian traditions and made sacrifices at the Apis bull at the old capital of Memphis. This made him immensely popular. He was formally crowned Pharaoh on or about November 14, 332 B.C. He sailed down the River Nile and at the place where it meets the Mediterranean Sea, he founded a new city that he called Alexandria. It is said that Alexander had brought with him loads of architects and engineers. However, he gave his own ideas for the layout of the new city. Alexander went on to found about 20 such towns and cities all over Asia and called them all Alexandria. The Egyptian Alexandria, however, was his favourite and became one of the most important cities of the ancient world. Even today, more than 2,000 years later, Alexandria is still the second largest city of Egypt after Cairo and is still known as, 'The Pearl of the Mediterranean.'

While Alexandria was under construction, the Macedonians marched back up the Mediterranean coast and then north-east through modern Syria and crossed the river Euphrates into Mesopotamia.

While in Egypt, in March 331 B.C., Alexander with a group of soldiers set off on a 300-miles trip along the Mediterranean coast and then south into the scorching North African desert towards a tiny town called Siwah. The purpose of this trip was to consult the oracle of the god Zeus-Ammon, a fusion of two important Greek and Egyptian gods. It was a dangerous trip. Darius could have attacked when he was away or Alexander could have endangered his own life in one of the frequent sandstorms. No one knew why he had made this trip or what questions about the future he had asked at the oracle. Alexander came out of the shrine, brimming with confidence and forever afterwards claimed a close relationship with Amun, the Egyptian god.

The Egyptians worshipped Alexander as a living god, because he was now their Pharaoh (though he was not actually crowned). All the Pharaohs were looked upon as divine.

Throughout his life, Alexander was a controversial figure. He was loved, hated and feared by friend and foe alike. However, his claim to be god has been the most discussed about. He was one of the first Greeks to be worshipped as a god in his own lifetime.

Four years later in 327 B.C., in Bactra (in modern-day Afghanistan) Alexander told his court to pay 'proskynesis' or homage to him. His new Persian subjects accepted it. They considered such homage as a mark of respect shown to a superior. As Alexander was at that point the Great King of Persia, there was no one more superior to him. His Macedonian and Greek subjects, however, termed it as a religious act and declined to obey. They did not consider Alexander to be a god like Zeus or Apollo. But Alexander's main intention for demanding homage was to make his Macedonian, Greek and Persian subjects feel equal within his own Empire.

Yet some ancient writers have said that in 324 B.C., Alexander asked every one to worship him as a god. There is no proof of this but by then Alexander was riding high in confidence, thinking himself to be unbeatable and hence in effect a god.

'I Will Not Demean Myself by Stealing Victory Like a Thief'

Coming back to his conquests, Alexander was ready to lead his army out of Egypt towards new invasions in the east and a final showdown with Darius. A revolt back at home in Greece had been easily crushed by Antipater, Alexander's regent in Macedon. Alexander was now prepared to fulfill his lifetime ambition and complete his capture of the strong Persian Empire.

As he usually did, he left a garrison of Macedonian soldiers behind, but happily left the running of the country mostly with the Egyptians. The Egyptians loved him even more for this and, unlike the other states of his enormous kingdom, Alexander never had any trouble in Egypt.

Alexander's heart was now set on capturing the great cities in the heart of the Persian Empire, which had held an attraction for him from childhood—with their exotic names such as Babylon, Susa, Persepolis and Pasargadae.

Darius, however, had been busy reorganizing the army, getting ready to confront Alexander again. He had wanted to stop the advance of the Macedonian army at the River Tigris, but Alexander managed to cross this. The decisive battle between the two armies finally took place in a vast, hot and dusty plain at Gaugamela, near modern-day Iraq.

On the eve of the battle, Darius's wife—still a prisoner in the Macedonian camp—died while giving birth to Darius's child. Darius was very upset when he got the news. He sent Alexander a peace offering.

Darius offered to surrender a third of his entire empire. He agreed that Alexander could keep all the land he had conquered, including Phoenicia, Syria and Egypt. He also offered 30,000 talents in cash if Alexander would release his family. If Alexander had accepted this generous offer, he could have returned to Macedonia with pride and would have been held in great acclaim for all his great conquests. However, Alexander being

Alexander would not be satisfied with anything less than the entire empire of Darius. So he wrote back to Darius that just as the earth could not be imagined with two suns, so the continent of Asia could not have two kings.

The next morning Alexander, while surveying the Persian army, was in for a shock. Darius had around 220,000 infantry and 30, 000 cavalry while Alexander had only 40,000 infantry and 7,000 cavalry. Alexander spent several hours riding around on Bucephalus, taking stock of the army formations of the enemy. His general Parmenio suggested a surprise attack in the night, but Alexander rejected the idea saying that he wanted to have an honourable victory and not one by cheating. He told his general, 'I will not demean myself by stealing victory like a thief.'

And true to his word, by using better tactics and cavalry skills, Alexander fought against all odds and won the battle. Darius again fled.

Darius's name as a Great King was beginning to lose its sheen while Alexander's popularity rose to its zenith. And as he marched with his army further east, many cities welcomed him with open arms. One of the most glorious cities in the whole of the ancient world, Babylon, threw open its gates for Alexander and his army where they enjoyed a month's well-earned rest. While his men enjoyed themselves, Alexander spent his time learning Babylonian astrology.

Persian Way of Life

Alexander next stopped at Susa, 375 miles south-east of Babylon and another of the Great King's palatial cities. The local satrap came out to greet him as he proceeded through the Royal road. He brought Alexander gifts including a herd of camels and a dozen elephants. Then he formally surrendered the city. Here Alexander sat on the imperial golden throne for the first time. Touring the Royal Palace and treasury, Alexander's eyes popped out on seeing the riches. Apart from a fantastic hoard of gold and silver coins, there were heaps and heaps of gold plates and jewellery. Besides these, he discovered the finest ancient tapestries and rooms full of luxurious furnishings. Right in the centre of it all stood the King's legendary throne with its exquisite golden canopy.

A few hundred miles further east was the holy city of Persepolis, the religious capital of the Persian Empire. More wealth was found in the royal palaces of Persepolis. There the wealth of gold, silver, jewels and other treasures were so great that Alexander needed a huge number of camels to transport them all. Then Alexander had the palaces burnt to the ground. No one knows why Alexander decided to destroy Persepolis. He lost the respect of the Persians. He lost all chances of the Persians accepting him willingly as their new king. It is said that Alexander soon repented his action and gave orders to put out the fire.

However, the Persians, it is said, did not consider Alexander a hero or a liberator, but as Iskander—'the thief' who stole their country. He is known by this name in Iran even today.

Alexander was naturally a generous person and grew more so as his fortune increased. He was displeased if any one refused his presents. How magnificent he was in enriching his friends and those who attended on him can be seen in a chiding letter written by Olympias, in which she tells him that he should reward and honour his subjects in a moderate way.

Alexander moved on. He needed to capture Darius and force him to abdicate. He wanted to catch him alive, force him to step down and officially hand over the empire. Then the people would accept him as a lawful successor to the Great King. However, as Alexander travelled north towards Ecbatana in 330 B.C, he heard that Darius had fled east toward Bactria. Alexander thought of a plan.

He decided to reorganize his army. He felt he could no longer trust the Greek allied soldiers (the soldiers who came from Greek states other than Macedon) to be loyal to him. Now that he had freed the cities of the Asia Minor and Darius was largely defeated, he did not require their services. Those who wanted to leave were given their pay and allowed to go. Those who remained were paid three talents, which was a huge sum, for their loyalty.

Having rearranged his troops, Alexander set out in haste in search of Darius. He covered 450 miles in three weeks. However, his efforts proved futile.

News reached him that Darius had been dethroned by a distant relative, Bessus, who was also one of his generals at Gaugamela. Bessus had proclaimed himself as king and claimed that he had imprisoned Darius.

Alexander chose 500 of his toughest men and coaxed them to attempt an all-night chase through the Iranian desert in order to catch up with Bessus and save Darius. They almost caught up with him, but all they found was a hastily abandoned camp-site, with a single wagon. There was a strange moaning coming out of the wagon. It was Darius, barely alive.

As the Macedonian army was approaching, Bessus had stabbed Darius with javelins. A Macedonian soldier found him just on the brink of death and gave him water. Darius was dead, by the time Alexander arrived. Alexander sent his body back to be buried in the royal cemetery at Persepolis. After that he continued his journey to capture Bessus.

With the death of Darius, Alexander's soldiers hoped that they would all be going home. They were weary of crossing thousands of miles of desert. They had been away from their families for four years. They had taken over the capital cities and Darius had been given a royal burial. It took Alexander all his efforts to convince his men to stay on with him.

Alexander was slowly getting attracted to the Persian way of dressing. First he tried out Darius's head band and then put on some fashionable oriental robes. He even experimented with the eyeliner and mascara, very much a craze among the Persian men at that time. Soon he persuaded his friends to wear Persian clothes and even began decking out the Macedonian horses in elaborately decorated Persian harness.

Alexander's empire was now huge, extending thousands and thousands of miles. There were not enough Macedonian troops to take care of his entire empire. So he would have to get the Persians to support him if he wanted to rule the whole of his kingdom peacefully. In order to be accepted by the Persians, he was ready to act as a Persian if necessary. He also married Roxanne, the daughter of the defeated Sogdian chieftain whose support he wanted to acquire.

Most of Alexander's close friends did not have any objection to the new fashion at court. However, the old officers who had once fought for King Philip were conservative and stuck to the traditional Macedonian way of doing things. They were of the opinion that it should be the Persians who should adopt Macedonian ways. Some of his followers, who were annoyed at Alexander's persuasion to follow the lifestyle of the defeated Persians, plotted against him. A group of royal attendants who had conspired against him were put down ruthlessly.

To keep his army in good spirits and to take their mind off their worries, Alexander organized several feasts and all-night drinking parties. He also encouraged his soldiers to marry Persian girls. By these measures, he aimed to make them forget their craving for their homes in Macedonia and to look at the Persian campaign as part of their life.

For the next three years, Alexander stayed on in the north of the vast Persian Empire, chasing Bessus and crushing rebellions in remote parts of the country. Bactria was in the north-eastern corner of the Persian Empire (Kandahar in modern Afghanistan) and it was a mountainous place. Alexander had to face a lot of problems here. Bessus was clever not to fight Alexander directly. He used the mountains as cover, forcing the Macedonians into dangerous passes. He would then attack them. The Macedonians had the double job of facing the local tribesmen also, who would suddenly emerge from the mountain areas and attack them. Even some of the local satraps who had surrendered to him would rise in revolt as soon as he had left the scene.

Soldier Trouble

Alexander's men suffered from frostbite, snow-blindness, altitude sickness and sore feet. The Macedonian army was frustrated and the expedition was going to take more than a year. When complaints started pouring in, Alexander began to suspect the continued loyalty of his men. He was worried. His anxiety made him act mercilessly. The next to receive his wrath was General Parmenio, who was then serving as the local ruler at Ecbatana in western Persia. Parmenio did not approve of Alexander's new Persian ways and this irritated the king. Alexander wanted to do away with him, but Parmenio was a highly respected officer and had fought wars even during the time of King Philip.

He was still a popular figure in the Macedonian army. So he could not be arrested without reason. Alexander, however, soon got an opportunity.

One day a young man approached Philotas, the son of Parmenio. He passed on a rumour he had heard concerning a plot to kill Alexander. Philotas promised the man he would warn Alexander, but for some reason he did not do so. When Alexander finally heard about it, he used this chance to arrest Philotas and then tortured him until he 'confessed' to plotting with his father against Alexander. Philotas was stoned to death. Alexander sent two of his men immediately to Parmenio with a letter. While he was opening the letter, he was hacked to death as per orders from Alexander.

Unfortunately, these stern acts only added to the resentment and suspicion among the ordinary soldiers. Alexander thought of another plan to find out what was on their minds. He allowed them to write letters to their homes and dispatched all the letters through couriers. Half way through, he would call them back and collect the letters. He would read all the letters to know what his men were telling about him. Any one who had written uncomplimentary things about him was soon transferred to a special unit in the army, which he reserved for the most dangerous and hopeless missions.

Alexander's treks to catch Bessus took him beyond Bactria into the land of Sogdiana (known today as Uzbekistan and Tajikistan). In 329 B.C., with the help of the local Sogdian ruler Spitamenes, Alexander finally captured and killed Bessus. Spitamenes, however, soon changed his idea of being friends with the Macedonians. Soon Alexander had another enemy in Spitamenes, who proved a very tricky opponent. It was only after a lengthy campaign that, by 327 B.C., he finally conquered the entire area. Here again Alexander's prowess as a great general was evident as he tackled the small-scale surprise attacks of guerrilla warfare with skill.

In the meanwhile the Macedonian army was weary of Alexander's distrust of his soldiers. One night during a late-night dinner party, Alexander got drunk. In the drunken state, he claimed to be the greatest of all, much above his father and even Heracles and Achilles. Most of the Macedonians were too scared of Alexander to disagree. However, Alexander's trusted friend Cleitus, the man who had saved his life at the Granicus, was not going to remain silent. He was aware of the discontent among the Macedonian soldiers and spoke out. He accused Alexander of spilling the blood of a large number of Macedonians for his own ends.

Alexander, who was not one to take criticism, had heard enough and he lost his temper. The two men were at each other and in the fray that followed, Alexander murdered his friend. A dreadful silence followed; the men gathered there did not know what to do. The moment he saw the outcome of his anger, Alexander was filled with remorse. He knew he had done a terrible mistake and every one had witnessed it. He hastily went to his tent and sulked, refusing to eat. He told every one that he was starving to death to atone for his sin. His men were unhappy, but they knew that only Alexander could take them home. So they pleaded with him to come out and continue to be their leader. They agreed with him that he was King and Lord of all Asia.

When Alexander was camping in Sogdiana, a spring of water and a spring of oil gushed up close to his tent. Alexander, who was superstitious, thought that it meant that he was going to have trouble ahead. In fact it is the first mention of petroleum in all of Greek literature.

By 327 B.C. Alexander crushed the last pockets of opposition to his rule in Persia. He founded a fortified city in the north of Sogdiana called, 'Alexandria-the-Furthest.' He had to face one more local rebellious leader called Oxyartes. He had hidden himself in the mountains, with 30,000 men and enough supplies for two years. Alexander chose 300 men and ordered them to climb the cliff face on the far side of Oxyartes's fortress. In this way they would be hidden from view. The climb was tough and many men fell to their death. The survivors, however, stood high on the summit and Oxyartes was surprised to see these men in the morning, looking down into his camp. As the sun shone, the men took out a white sheet that Alexander had asked them to carry with them and waved it in the wind. Oxyartes, totally taken unawares, surrendered his fortress without fight.

Alexander married Roxanne, Oxyartes's daughter. Many of his supporters thought he would now rest, but Alexander got his army back on the march. He also imposed another Oriental custom on his soldiers. For the Persians it was normal to greet any important person, by bowing before them. The Greeks never bowed before any mortal, even if he was a king. They bowed only before gods. Alexander announced that all the Macedonian officers would henceforth bow down before him as Great King. The Macedonians were horrified. They found it humiliating and offensive to the gods. However, they dared not oppose.

One person, however, had the guts to refuse. This was Aristotle's nephew Callisthenes, one of the historians who had been brought along on the trip and a very popular person in the army. Alexander controlled his anger and resisted his temptation to kill Callisthenes then and there. However, he soon concocted charges against him and Callisthenes was sentenced to death.

Conquest of India

Before the year was out in the spring of 327 B.C., he crossed the Hindu Kush Mountains (on the border between modern Afghanistan and Pakistan) again. He had crossed it once in pursuit of Bessus in spring 329 B.C. The Greeks believed that the world was surrounded by a water body known as 'Ocean,' which lay beyond India. Alexander was keen to see this water and the land of India. The Greeks had no idea how big India was. For them, it was a place surrounded by myth and fable. Alexander somehow persuaded his men to go on, regaling them with strange stories that the travellers had spread about India.

Alexander divided his troops of 100,000 men. One group under his friend, Hephaestion, went east through Khyber Pass towards the River Indus, while Alexander headed towards the hilly area in the north. The army that Alexander had now was far different from the one he had started with seven years earlier. Only some 15,000 Macedonians remained; the rest were all Persians and others forced to fight for Alexander. He recruited 30,000 strong Persian youths and trained them in Macedonian warfare. Alexander's plan was to replace the aging Macedonians with this new group. So it was obvious that Alexander had many more campaigns in his agenda.

By spring 326 B.C., he had conquered the northern Indian states and met up with Hephaestion at the River Indus. Alexander's army had to encounter a lot of hurdles during their travel through India. They were not used to the torrential monsoon rains, which poured continuously for days on end. Soaked to the skin, they had to trudge along through miles of stinking swamps, which were the breeding ground for mosquitoes. Many were down with malaria. Their weapons got rusted in the damp air; their clothes got damaged in the hot climate; many of them suffered from infected foot, prickly heat and dysentery.

The army also had to fight one of the fiercest battles in the whole campaign. This was the Battle of the Hydaspes against Porus (the Greek version of Puru, Pururava or Parvata), the raja of the Pauravas. Alexander's eye fell on the vast lands of raja Porus and naturally they were his next target. Alexander sent a message, asking Porus to pay homage. Unlike Ambi, the king of Taxila who welcomed Alexander, Porus refused to submit to him.

Porus stood in defiance with a 50,000-strong army and 85 trained war elephants. It was the most fearsome-looking army that Alexander had ever met. The two armies met on either side of the river Hydaspes (River Jhelum). It was monsoon season and the river was in full flood. So Alexander could not cross. He left part of his army behind as a reserve force and with the rest went upstream to find a crossing place. Alexander crossed the river and the two armies met. The battle turned out to be a bloodbath as well as a mud bath. The elephants trampled to death many Macedonians while a few got stuck on their tusks. Some were picked up by the huge elephants in their trunks and were dashed to the ground. The terrifying trumpeting noises of the elephants reverberated in the air.

However, finally Alexander's men found a way to tackle them. They attacked the men atop the elephants with arrows and javelins. Cutting at the feet and trunks of the elephants, they drove them to the brink of madness. In their frenzy the elephants began to trample the Indian soldiers. In the meanwhile, Alexander's reserve forces crossed the river to attack Porus from behind. Things were falling in favour of Alexander and soon Porus was defeated. It was a great victory, perhaps Alexander's finest, but it cost him many lives, including one that was dear to him: Bucephalus, his horse that was with him for twenty years, died of wounds received in the battle.

Roman historian Arrian describes the capture of Porus. Porus had suffered many arrow wounds in the battlefield and had lost his sons, who all chose death in battle rather than surrender. Alexander, seeing the king held captive, his body in chains, asked him, 'What am I supposed to do with you?'

'Treat me the way one king treats another,' was the brave response.

Alexander was impressed by his personality and treated him generously. His kingdom was returned to him and additional lands were also gifted to him.

The defeat of Porus was just the beginning of his conquest of India. His troops, however, were tired, with continuous marching in rain-sodden clothes and sleeping in hammocks hung from trees to avoid being bitten by snakes. Alexander tried to convince them that the ocean was near. But they had heard stories of savage tribes, waiting to attack. Their belief in him was waning. The army realized that Alexander had no intention of going back. Conquering new lands had become a way of life for him. He wanted to win more and more. Some of the soldiers had been with him from the time he had set out, which was about eight years, and had marched with him for about 17,000 miles. Naturally they wanted to go home, meet their families and relax.

In June 326 B.C. the army moved east again to the River Hyphasis, now known as the Beas. There was flat land and no sight of the ocean. Rumour spread that the Indian tribe was waiting for them on the other side with more than 4,000 trained elephants. So the soldiers rebelled—they just threw down their weapons and refused to go any further. No amount of coaxing by Alexander would change their minds. His speeches just could not stir them. A brave soldier called Coenus even countered Alexander's words saying that above any thing else, a successful man ought to know—'when to stop.'

For the first time Alexander was facing a full-scale mutiny. He sulked for two days in his tent. The army, however, was adamant. They were packing their things for the return journey. Reluctantly, Alexander decided to head back home. He turned back to the River Hydaspes, his conquests finally coming to an end.

The Gruelling Journey Back Home

Before they began their return journey, the Macedonians set up 12 huge statues of the Greek gods on the banks of the river. They also left an enormous obelisk with the message,

'ALEXANDER STOPPED HERE'

Some months earlier, Alexander had ordered the construction of a huge fleet of more than 1,000 ships. There were about 120,000 people together with women, children, animals and quite a lot of luggage also. The exhausted army finally was ready to sail. Some 8,000 soldiers sailed down the Rivers Hydaspes and Indus towards the Arabian Sea. For the rest, there was no room in the boats. So they, led by Hephaistion and Craterus, walked down the riverbanks on foot.

At the start the journey was uneventful, but Alexander's battles were not yet over. There were several powerful tribes who attacked them. Their march turned out to be one long continuous battle. The Macedonians slaughtered thousands as they fought their way to the sea. At one point Alexander was engaged in a battle with the Malli (modern day Multan) people. His soldiers were hesitant to join. So Alexander climbed up a wall and into the town. He urged his people to follow, but found himself alone. He fought until an arrow pierced his chest. His lung was punctured and his life was in danger. Luckily, the Macedonian soldiers entered the town and saved him. He was seriously ill for weeks and was confined in his tent.

Gradually Alexander recovered. The travel down the river resumed and the Macedonian army reached the mouth of the Indus in the summer of 325 BC. Here, he stopped to build an entire system of docks and harbours so that the fleet could be overhauled. Hephaistion was left in charge of this. One group of older soldiers had already been sent west from the Indus toward Central Persia.

Alexander then went off with a smaller fleet to explore the coastal area further downstream. Initially everything went well. Alexander's men were able to keep close to the shore with no danger of getting lost. However, the going soon got tougher with mountainous terrains. To avoid this terrain, Alexander and his men ventured inland and into the worst part of the most inhospitable Gedrosian (or Makran) Desert. They soon got into a sandstorm and there was shortage of drinking water and other supplies. Many of his members suffered from heatstroke while wagons of animals sank in deep sand dunes. It was hell for his soldiers, who were bitten by venomous snakes and pricked by poisonous plants. His fleet, without him, sailed down the Indus to the sea and then west along the Arabian Sea and into the Persian Gulf.

It is not known why Alexander chose this route back to Persia while he could easily have taken the northerly and safer route that was taken by Craterus and his older troops. May be, Alexander wanted to be the first to walk through the Gedrosian Desert. The trip, however, was a total disaster. Thousands of women and children travelling with the army were washed away by flash floods. Many in the army too lost their lives. Only a quarter of the 85,000 people who had started off with Alexander remained.

Alexander, however, was determined to succeed. Now to continue with their journey, Alexander planned to coordinate with the fleet led by his childhood friend Nearchus of Crete. The army would march along the shore, digging wells to provide water. The fleet would sail close to the shore with four month's supplies. The first part of the way through the present Baluchistan in southern Pakistan had plenty of food and water. However, then the army was forced inland by the mountains and their contact with the fleet was lost.

Men, women and children travelled through the fertile land, but soon it was all hot sand with no water. At one place, a soldier found a little water. He scooped it up in his helmet and gave to Alexander to drink. Alexander was thirsty but he refused to drink, knowing his men's plight. Then there was torrential rain, which swept away everything in their path. The rains were followed by sand storms. Alexander lost his way, but managed to get back to the sea. The rest of the army followed and after two months, they reached the relative safety of Pura in southern Persia. Many of his men had died of thirst and heat.

In Carmania, southern Persia, Alexander met Craterus and the troops he had sent home. He also met with

Nearchus's fleet in March 324 B.C. The reunion called for huge celebrations.

However, Alexander was ill at ease. Stories were being circulated about revolts and even plots against his life. Alexander came to know what had been going on at the heart of the Persian Empire in his absence. He heard that many of the men he had appointed as satraps were indulging in excess, spending extravagantly, stealing money from the royal coffers. One of his oldest friends, Harpalus, the Grand Imperial Treasurer, had run off with a large part of Alexander's personal wealth. Alexander was furious, but tried to set things right. He summoned all the satraps and senior officers to Carmania. There he arrested most of them and executed some. There was a reign of terror unleashed by Alexander, who was brutal in his treatment of the wrong-doers. In their places he appointed new satraps, including a large number of Persian noble men.

The harsh experience in the desert had unnerved Alexander. The undutiful behaviour of his own people also disturbed him. He was afraid more trouble would follow. So he decided to be generous and cancelled the debts of all the soldiers. He even sent home some Greek men who had fought for the Persians as mercenaries. He also passed orders to all Greek cities that they should receive these Greek men, forgive them and treat them well. Actually these people had once fought against their own cities and had fled to join Alexander. This order caused a great uproar in Greece. Alexander's second decree was that he was now a god. Alexander had achieved a great deal in his conquests and he decided that human honours were not equal to crown his greatness. He believed that with his conquest of Asia and being the Pharaoh of Egypt, he was definitely above the human race. However, many of his politicians did not approve of the announcement. Some were furious while some thought it was a joke.

Next Alexander held a mass wedding. He got about 80 of his Macedonian followers to marry Persian noblewomen. Also 10,000 of his troops tied the knot with Persian women with his blessings. He gave each couple a gift of money. He himself married two women, belonging to the Persian royal house. Alexander's idea was the formation of a Macedonian-Persian group who would rule and fight for his empire in the future. Many Macedonians, however, did not take kindly to being forced to adopt eastern customs.

Alexander then travelled to Opis (modern-day Baghdad). In June 324 B.C., the army rebelled again. The revolt started when Alexander paid off 10,000 Macedonian soldiers and replaced them with the 30,000 Persian youth he had started to train in 327 B.C. Moreover, he asked the Macedonian soldiers to go home. These soldiers had hoped to return to Macedonia as war heroes, alongside their emperor. Without Alexander, they would not receive any honour in their country; instead they would be sidelined as retired oldies. They also realized that Macedonia was no longer the important place that it had been. Alexander's interest now lay in Babylon. So the soldiers put down their weapons and began their protest. Alexander pacified them and held a banquet of reconciliation for his Macedonian soldiers. Those who mutinied were given seats of honour near him and were even allowed to drink from the royal wine bowl. He also gave them the Persian title, 'Kinsmen.' The soldiers were made to feel special and many of them were reassured. Alexander sent them home as planned.

Final Days

The last year of Alexander's life was tough. Continuous fighting, the revolt of his army on two occasions, the ordeal in the desert and the serious wound he had received in India drained him of his energy. Although he did not want to go back to Macedonia, he did not want to settle in Babylon also. Yet he was not one to sit still and had great plans for more adventure.

In summer 324 B.C., he travelled to his summer retreat in the hill city of Ecbatana. There he threw one of his lavish parties to celebrate the annual festival of Dionyus, god of wine. Suddenly his best friend and companion Hephaestion collapsed on the ground and was found to be suffering from fever. In spite of the doctor's efforts, Hephaestion died a few days later. Alexander was devastated. Grief-stricken, he cut off his hair in mourning and ordered the manes and tails of royal horses to be trimmed as well. He banned playing of all musical instruments in court till further notice.

He embalmed Hephaestion's body and sent it off to Babylon for a grand and extravagant funeral. Alexander took his revenge for his friend's death in the cruellest possible way. He executed the doctor for failing to save Hephaestion.

The death of his friend was a real blow to Alexander, who became increasingly depressed and took to heavy drinking. However, he also threw himself into work, planning new projects such as the invasion of Arabia and even an attack on Carthage in the Mediterranean. His new campaign targeted a tribe called the Cossaei, who controlled the mountain area and levied a toll on those who wanted to pass the area to reach Babylon or Susa. The Persian rulers had been paying the toll, unable to tackle the tribe. Alexander decided to subdue them, and after 41 days of fighting he totally wiped them out. He was 32 years old and had so far lived a charmed life.

In spring 323 B.C. Alexander returned to Babylon. It is said that seers had warned him not to enter the city facing the setting sun. There was impregnable swampland west of the city. He paid no heed to their words and entered the city from the east. There were some other bad omens. A sudden gust of wind blew away his sun hat wrapped with the royal ribbon and it got caught in the reeds next to the tomb of a long-dead king. Another time, while Alexander was on his feet inspecting the troops, a mad man sat on his throne. It is possible that writers have exaggerated some of these warnings to heighten the drama surrounding Alexander's death.

On May 29, 323 B.C. Alexander held a banquet in honour of his admiral Nearchus of Crete, who was planning a voyage around Arabia. He was feeling a bit low and when he was on his way to bed, some friends persuaded him to join another late-night party. He woke up the next day with a fever caused by typhus or malaria. His condition worsened and he was incapacitated. He ordered his officers to remain close. He gave his royal ring to his general Perdiccas, so that the ruling of the empire and other important matters would continue to receive his approval. On June 10, his friends who stayed by his bed-side, asked him, 'To whom do you leave your empire?'

'To the strongest,' he replied. And with those words he died.

After Alexander's death in Babylon, in 323 B.C., his body was embalmed. The following year, it was taken under a huge escort to the royal cemetery at Aegae in Macedon. However, some people said that Alexander had wanted to be buried at the oracle of Amun in Egypt—which he had visited in 331 B.C. So finally he was buried in Egypt. His exact burial site has never been discovered.

Though Alexander's death is attributed to fever, aggravated by heavy drinking or due to malaria, many even argue that he was deliberately poisoned. And the suspicion falls on Aristotle and Antipater, both of whom had antagonised Alexander with their disloyalties. They both disliked his favourable treatment of the Persians. However, this could not be proved.

In his short span of life (he was now 33 years old) Alexander achieved much. His empire stretched from the Adriatic Sea in the west to what is Pakistan in the east, and from Egypt in Africa in the south to modern Uzbekistan in Central Asia in the north. He had led his army across mountains, deserts, rivers and seas and he had won victory after victory against impossible odds—

—all in a little more than ten years. So it is clear why he has been called Alexander, the Great.

However, Alexander was not good at looking after his empire. There was continuous bickering amongst people who wanted to inherit it. At his death, he left the empire in the hands of an unborn son by his wife Roxanne and his mentally ill half-brother, Philip Arrhidaeus. Neither of them was a suitable successor. Perdiccas tried to rule on their behalf. However, by 270 B.C., after Perdiccas was murdered, the entire kingdom broke up into three separate kingdoms—Egypt, Western Asia and Macedon. Finally each was conquered by the next great imperial power, Rome.

Alexander was great as a leader, but he was also cruel. It is said that he was responsible for the death of three-quarters of a million people.

However, in his 32 years he has created the greatest military records in history. He was tactful and effective in adapting to enemy tactics. He always knew how to exploit a weakness. As a leader, he was unsurpassed. He knew how to select the governors and obtain loyalty from them. His people may not have loved him, but he ruled them by invoking the appropriate balance of fear and respect.

In spite of all his shortcomings, Alexander's influence on the development of the world is noteworthy. He founded about 70 cities and enabled the Greek culture to spread in the East. Trade and social communication between East and West opened up.

Some people considered him to be a noble conqueror who brought two major civilizations together while to some others he was a blood-thirsty monster who brought suffering and pain to people. However, all agree that few men have changed the course of history as Alexander did.